I0224679

Walk on Air:
Haiku over the Hudson

Poems for mindfulness

poems by

Deirdre Cornell

Finishing Line Press
Georgetown, Kentucky

Walk on Air:
Haiku over the Hudson

Poems for mindfulness

ACKNOWLEDGMENTS

I would like to acknowledge all the local residents who care for our Hudson
River Valley in so many ways. I would especially like to thank those who
make possible the Walkway Over the Hudson. As a segment of The Hudson
Valley Rail Trail, the Walkway belongs to the New York State Office of
Parks, Recreation and Historical Preservation and the New York State
Bridge Authority. At the Walkway Over the Hudson organization, Elizabeth
Waldstein, Geoff Brault and Theresa Sanchez provided much-appreciated
encouragement at just the right time. Cover art is by Kathleen Monahan and
is reproduced with permission of The Friends of Walkway Over the Hudson
organization.

Caledonia Kearns suggested publishers. Marjorie Farrell and Marian Ronan
helped with editing. At Finishing Line Press, Christen Kincaid turned my
manuscript into a book with skill and patience. Elizabeth Maines McCleavy
supervised design.

Mike Leach, my guardian angel for all these years—thank you!

My parents and brother cultivate our family's roots in the Hudson Valley,
and my children keep me grounded. Deepest thanks go to my husband, a
steady and faithful walking partner.

Publisher: Leah Huete de Maines
Editor: Christen Kincaid
Cover Art: *Walkway Sunrise* by Kathleen Monahan
Author Photo: Kenney Gould
Cover Design: Elizabeth Maines McCleavy

Order online: www.finishinglinepress.com
also available on amazon.com

Author inquiries and mail orders:
Finishing Line Press
P. O. Box 1626
Georgetown, Kentucky 40324
U. S. A.

Table of Contents

for fellow walkers everywhere

Introduction

These poems arose from waking to beauty.

Growing up on the banks of the Hudson River, I took for granted its spectacular scenery. In 2009, a walking bridge (constructed from remains of the 1889 Poughkeepsie-Highland Railroad trestle) made possible new vantage points. The world's longest elevated pedestrian bridge, the Walkway Over the Hudson spans the river for 1.28 miles at an altitude of 212 feet above water. Once I overcame my fear of heights, I appreciated familiar landscape as never before. And I am not alone: half a million visitors come to the bridge each year. We walk, jog, ride, skate, run, march and rollerblade from one shore to the other, in silence and solidarity.

In walking, the lesson that came to me was mindfulness. In writing, the literary form was the haiku. A three-lined poem with set numbers of syllables, the haiku (Japanese in origin) is often used for poetry about nature. Its musing, breath-taken quality seemed particularly suited to describing the Hudson River's panorama and changing seasons. I soon found my thoughts drifting to life and love; and I was drawn to the cast of characters (human and canine) of my fellow sojourners. Walking brought me into the present moment, grateful and awake.

I hope these poems will awaken readers to beauty—whether in the Hudson Valley, or elsewhere—and to the present moment, as well.

Deirdre Cornell
Hudson River Valley
November 2020

One brave, little boat
Learning to float—that is me:
Happy. Terrified.

The Mighty Hudson

Sky, you fill my eyes
The way water quenches thirst:
Liquid sun, pouring.

Did you see? Rosy
Skies melding into water—
The river at dusk?

Just at the edge, light.
Where mountains meet horizon—
Bright where light meets dark.

I'm walking on air!
Skimming treetops, riding waves—
Gliding glad blue sky.

It rarely happens,
But it did: I walked, alone,
No one else in sight.

When I am away
Tides rush, jealous, through my dreams
To caress my sleep

I hear the train horn,
And wonder: in your dark house,
Do you hear it too?

Flat harmonica
Horn gripped in train-engine teeth:
"Don't come near. Danger."

Counting railroad cars:
Rectangle freight containers
Boxed steel and color.

The flag, at half-mast
In honor of those who fell
So that we might rise

One tiny blue tug
Pushes huge barges upstream—
No waves in its wake!

After the rain, sun.
Before the sun was the rain.
Rain + sun = rainbow.

A wedge of water:
The wake of a dayliner
Laboring upstream

To whoever owns
A little boat named "Get Free:"
I am still trying.

Water sweeps away
Treasure, garbage, accidents.
All in one river.

A sight for sore eyes:
The view opens wide, wider
Shining—river—light

Sunset, a sliver
Of rosy ribbon, lying
Along waves of steel.

Emerald mountains
Silver waves, gold horizon.
Riches beyond wealth.

A diamond shimmers
On the edge of every wave,
Yours for the taking—

Silver-crested waves
Shine, a million diamond rings
Set in platinum

Is there no limit?
It feels endless: sky trees wind /
The river's long tread.

The breeze ripples waves
Into fine ribs on water
One fluid body.

A loud, brash speedboat
Leaves no white curls in its wake
Only lots of noise

Praise, now, the floating
Log, the one that does its job
So well: showing up.

Did you see the birds?
Did you count six sharp-tipped wings
Slicing through white clouds?

Early dawn, seagulls
Let loose their temper tantrums.
Petulant children!

Ev'ning comes. Seagulls'
Cawing stops. On riverbanks
Birdsong takes its place

Hawk: wings tilt one way
Then another—elegant
In pursuit of prey.

Birds trees sky mountain—
The river, bursting with life.
Like fam'ly, like kin.

Clouds moving quickly
To other skies, far-off lands,
Too fast to follow.

Stretch marks on water:
So this is what it feels like
When a river scars

Storm King, Mount Beacon—
The Mighty Hudson's shoulders.
Muscles ripple: waves.

First Nations called it
"The River that Flows Both Ways."
Sweet home; salty tears.

Henry Hudson dipped
Fingers in living water.
Marveled at these cliffs.

Kingston: the king's town
New York's first state capital—
Now, hipster heaven.

Spread for all to see,
The city of Poughkeepsie—
Its grit and glory.

Ulster, I head back
To your rolling, deep green hills
So glad to live here.

Homebody, homemade
Bring it home, home run, home stretch,
No place like…homesick.

Of all the places
I love, I love most the place
That most broke my heart.

Newburgh: on track rails
We learned to flatten nickels
Under raging wheels.

An estuary:
Cradle for the river young.
Waves rock, back and forth.

This view can't be bought,
Even for a million bucks.
Enjoy it, for free.

Places must exist
As breathtaking as this one
But…don't hold your breath!

So what's the big deal?
Only the most gorgeous view
In the entire world.

Trail, town, bridge: I love
To walk on and on…spacious,
Our Hudson Valley.

Love

Strange, how it rises,
Unbidden, after so long.
Passion: a swift flame.

My body, on fire
Missing you, both day and night.
When will you come home?

When the hours pass
And I still have not seen you
The dark grows darker.

I don't want to think
What would I do without you
But…I have to ask.

I missed you so much
I had to go for a walk.
My body, burning.

When will you and I
Fin'lly get it right: restless,
But at the same time?

My skin was on fire.
Limbs restless and heart ablaze.
Come with me next time.

If you look for me
I am not so hard to find.
But…are you looking?

Walking into day,
The hours take care of themselves.
Night's what must be filled.

It has been so long.
Parted from you, my own fault.
Please, please: forgive me.

Wait for me! I shout.
Can you even hear my voice?
You, so far ahead.

Birds sing of love lost.
Waves weep their way to shore.
I walk without you.

Where are you, blue eyes?
A perfect sky reminds me:
Why are you not here?

There you are again
Just when I thought I'd lost you.
Playing hide and seek.

The man that I love
Stands at the gate, still waiting
For me to come home.

I have been away
All these many days and months.
Yet, you take me back.

How can I make it?
Exhaustedsweatythirsty
You pull me along.

Mine, your noble heart!
You offered, so I took it—
Greedily, both hands.

When you pledged your love—
No exchanges or returns—
I stole a bargain!

The love of my life
Walks by my side. No complaints—
At least, not today.

From that moment on
(When you joined me on the bridge),
I've never looked back.

Who would have thought it?
At fifty, falling in love
With my own husband.

Will you walk with me?
Turn your gaze tow'rd the same shore,
Stroll with steady steps?

All I want is you.
I think, now—now, I'm ready.
Take my hand; let's see.

Slowly, slowly, come
To the bridge and walk with me.
There's plenty of time.

On the Bridge

Step out. Cross over
Turn challenge into pleasure
Walk, run, ride, or skate.

Roller blades, skateboards
Bicycles and tricycles
All sharing one bridge.

A stream of color—
Whirring gears, sharp bell, racers—
Bicycles flash past—

Fuji: Speedy. Schwinn:
Classic, sturdy. Bianchi:
Sleek, trim. Huffy: tough.

Low recumbent bike
Banner flying, gear in place.
Now *that's* a cool ride.

Fasten your helmets!
Careful of pedestrians!
No accidents, please!

Bridge ambassadors,
For your ready smiles, red vests,
And your time…thank you!

Cute, ugly, big, small
Fierce, tame, skittish, sociable:
Best friends on leashes.

Pit bulls, beagles, hounds
Cocker spaniels and poodles
Chihuahuas, Great Danes.

Greyhounds, retrievers
Vishlas, Dalmatians, corgies
Terriers, boxers.

Pure entertainment:
German shepherds and dachshunds
So much fun to watch—

Let's not forget mutts,
Beloved pets regardless
Of breed or pedigree!

One huge black poodle
One tiny one (in matching
Sweaters and haircuts)

Well-dressed terrier
In a luxury stroller
Wearing pink ribbons

People walk their dogs.
Or, maybe is it, instead...
Dogs walk their people?

Please, don't litter!
Leave the park as you found it:
Pristine. Holy, Clean.

Walks to be taken:
Vigorous. Relaxed. Eager.
Lazy. Delightful.

Old and young alike:
Bike, walk, run, jog, skate, or ride—
In good company.

Uncles aunts lovers
Toddlers moms dads teenagers
Friends and grandparents.

Radiant mother
Smiling dad, skipping children
Their joy, contagious!

A child holding hands
With both mother and father.
Learning how to walk.

Babies in buggies.
They sit there, snug companions
Along for the ride—

Runaway stroller!
Mischievous toddler sibling
Holds baby captive!

Cutest thing *ever*:
Sleeping baby in buggy
Sister at the helm.

Children learn to walk
Holding a slow, tender hand;
Too soon, they will run.

No! Don't say those words!
Don't you see the children cringe,
Hearing violent speech?

He crashed into me
A boy (six? seven?) years old
No apology.

Jagged rock, a mouth
Poised to bite children's bare feet
Scrambling on the shore.

Waving, to no one
In particular, to see—
Will someone wave back?

A nod or a smile—
Maybe even a hello—
Can go a long way.

A Chinese tour bus
Delivers fifty faces
From across the globe.

Today's languages:
Spanish (always), Dutch (I asked),
Hindi and English.

Overheard today:
German, Spanish, Japanese
Australian accents

Jamaican English
Spanish of many countries
Variety = spice!

Black coat, blond hair, purse
In the latest style. New York
Fashions on display.

"Christ! Look at this view!"
And, whipping out his cell phone,
He then stopped looking.

Old friends, chance meeting
Hugs, news, the latest events.
Promise: keep in touch.

Can you believe it?
Every person who passed by
Said hello or smiled!

New Year's Day surprise:
Two miniature donkeys
Trotting on the bridge.

"Ma, you talk too much.
Come on, just take the picture."
I took it for them.

Dating on the bridge:
"Are you a fan?" he asks her.
Of what? Since when?

Flip flops and sneakers
School shoes, work boots, ballet flats
But…foolish high heels.

Summer sandals: thongs
Leather / buckled / plain / beaded
Strappy / glittering

Dashikis, t-shirts,
Saris, yarmulkes, kerchiefs.
Sweatshirts, jogging suits.

Red sari, dampened.
In her other hand, sandals.
Barefoot in the rain.

Seasons

Morning: fog so thick
You can't see ahead of you.
One step at a time.

Winter on the bridge.
All is grey, icy. Pared down
By a knife-sharp wind.

Numbing to the touch—
Rails, gate, caboose, fence—frozen.
I can't feel my face.

Grey, and more grey: March
On the bridge. But now and then,
A flash of silver.

All of it must melt.
Sheets / blocks / shards / slivers be gone!
Winter into spring.

April, the weary
Flag flaps madly, and rude winds
Shove walkers across.

Silver, or murky
Golden, or grey—it depends:
Sunshine, or rainfall?

It has never been
Exactly the same, neither
Will it be again

Rain, rain and more rain
Silver coins fall, a treasure:
River abundance.

Birds, high overhead.
Wind stirs up small, rippling waves.
Spring, how I've missed you!

Sunshine on water.
At dusk, gold turns to silver.
Dawn, silver to gold.

Dark bodies of trees
Show off lacy green dresses.
Come, join the party!

Those who listen, hear.
The forest lives, breathes, sings, hums.
This river laughs, cries.

White wings o'er black waves
Tornado clouds form a fist
Poised to pound the earth

Tell me, how much green
Can eyes take in, how many
Verdant shades, tones, hues?

Surface flat, waves still.
For once, the flag hangs limp, sad.
No sign of a breeze.

My summertime prayer:
God, thank you for pink flowers
In bloom on the trail.

A red card'nal points
His tiny, solemn, scarlet hood
Straight up to heaven.

Little miracles,
Robins trill, chirp and warble.
No delight too small.

Velvet black feathers,
Iridescent, a grackle—
Eyes, two yellow beads

Twilight, birds chatter.
What do they gossip about?
Going on and on….

A red-winged blackbird!
It snaps into flight, soaring
O'er my lifted eyes.

Ninety-five degrees.
Pavement, hot as hell. Dog tongues
Drip, pant, beg, "Home. Home."

Quick! Thunder! Leave *now*—
Run, don't walk—get to safety
Before lightning strikes.

Luminous walking.
A column of light follows.
Bright sun, clear water.

Strange and wondrous rain:
A sudden golden downpour
While the sun still shines.

The glassy surface:
Its waves move as one body.
Is it blue? Or green?

Rose-colored sunset
Over rose-colored waters.
Summer. River. Dusk.

The coolness descends
Long-awaited. Welcome. Fresh.
All is peace. Soon, sleep.

Swallows slice a wedge
Into autumn sky. Seeking
Summer without end.

A garnet skirt, spread
Flickering, flaring, falling:
Japanese maple.

Autumn leaf harvest:
Ruby, jade, copper, gold, bronze—
A wealth of riches.

Lemon and pumpkin,
Pomegranate, cinnamon,
Colors of fall leaves.

Wildly dancing leaves
Crazy mad wind dashes o'er
landscape. October.

Autumn leaf, you fall
Without complaint or regret.
Teach me your secret!

November: slushy
Freezing rain turns into sleet.
Dark before sunset.

In broad daylight—moon!
Rising, huge, orange....Yet, taller,
Becoming smaller.

Noise goes quiet, throats
Catch, silent, as they arrive:
First snowflakes. First breath.

Look up, look around
Look across, beyond, within:
Beauty, everywhere.

Weary / Walking

You came from the light
Now go back to the light, turn
Your face to be blessed.

After a hard day
Walk as slowly as you want.
No one will object.

On this Walkway
You are not alone: friends, dogs,
Neighbors by your side.

Seeking your own way
You find yourself surrounded
By other trav'lers.

In this together:
Walking, running, and riding
Or even juggling!

When things go well, walk.
When things are not going well,
…All the more reason.

That tree, the same tree,
The one you look for each time—
It waits there for you.

You've made it this far.
So I ask you: "What comes next?"
You say, "I don't know."

Let it go. Walk. Breathe.
A thousand insults and hurts.
Take them to the bridge.

Anger fuels your gait.
Don't break your stride, keep walking!
They'll never catch up.

Why do you pretend
To be on the other side?
You are still here. *Still.*

Stay on the same side,
Or learn to live divided?
Neither: cross over.

"Where are you going?"
Silly question! There's only
Straight ahead—or back.

Just when you give up
You decide to discover
What you are made of.

Work—traffic—dinner—
hurry! Half a walk: better
Than no walk at all.

On the bridge again
It's as if I never left,
As if I *live* here.

I couldn't *not* hear:
"My father passed last week, and
Now I am alone."

Of course they walk slow—
So much weight on their shoulders!
Send them loving thoughts.

"I got results back,"
And she recounts the phone call
That might change her life.

Reaching middle age,
Next comes growing old. And *that's*
If we are *lucky.*

Inevitable.
I knew it had to happen
Yet…it still hurts me.

Too heavy to bear.
It was a long time ago.
Still, I carry it.

One year to the day,
You are gone. I miss you more
Than these words can say.

How can I go on?
I soldier blindly forward.
When will this all end?

When you can't go on…
Stop. Breathe. Look. Take it all in.
Beauty will save you.

Let it be enough.
Look above, below, around:
Diamonds, everywhere.

St. Paul had it right:
Grow rich in things that matter.
Love more. Worry less.

Walk fast, or walk slow.
It doesn't matter at all.
You will still get there.

Birds do it: fly high,
Trusting that it's possible.
You carry on, too.

Don't give up. Just try.
When you've spent all you came with,
Stop, and look around

Wider and wider,
Life dares us to new crossings.
No pity for fear.

Your life in your hands?
Don't be so sure. We are held
By hands we can't see.

God lives in the sky—
Or so we learned. Why argue
With a starry night?

Carrying children:
Even though they are not here,
I still feel their weight.

Pierced hearts: sons, daughters,
Parents alike—we are all
Learning how to love.

Children on my mind.
"Little ones, little problems.
Big ones, big problems."

Pray the young will find
Their way! Mind fills with worry,
Head with more grey hair

The kids are all grown up.
What I could do, I have done.
Time to walk alone.

Is this it, my life?
I have given it away
Way too many times!

When was the last time
You sat near water, doing
Nothing—just *being?*

"It is what it is…"
So, let it *be* what it is
It is. Let it be.

Oh, to be a boat!—
No need to apologize
For riding the tide.

Broke—spent—exhausted
Taking one step at a time.
Still walking my life.

I asked an old sage
For his best words of wisdom.
"Take care of your teeth."

The way of all flesh:
Bodies age. We diminish.
Seasons change. Tides ebb.

My body widens.
Ribcage expands, muscles sink.
Hair thins. Hips thicken.

Skin that loved the sun
Now pays the price: like paper
Wrinkled, mottled, lined.

Sore knees, tired back.
Same aches and pains, new complaints.
Blisters, weary feet.

Teeth ache. Bones stiffen.
Spine curves, body stoops. And yet…
At least I'm still here!

Jogging at ev'ning:
Am I running, or am I
Running out of time?

On asking myself,
"What did I get done today?"
I answer, "I walked."

How far can you go?
Do you have what it might take
To run the whole course?

Maybe it is true
That there is no finish line.
I like to think not.

Awakened

Everywhere, a breeze.
Wind moves clouds. Pay attention:
Wake up to your life.

After a long week
Of being away, I ask,
What took me so long?

The present moment:
Now—and there is only *now*—
Be *here*, on this bridge.

Reaching the midpoint
Of both my life and the bridge
At the same moment.

I glide over trees
Into sky, over water
On my way back home.

Look! Birds, overhead
Whether we see them, or not.
So...why not see them?

Here I am again—
How do the days pass so soon?
Once more on the bridge.

I almost did not
Notice one tremb'ling, green leaf.
Then I stopped. And did.

Right now: Start living.
Breathe in. Breathe out. That is all.
Your worries can wait.

I was not looking,
But it happened anyway:
The sun set, too soon.

Where's your inner voice?
The one that says, "Stop. Listen:
Wind, murmuring trees."

Inside the silence
Ask how to remain silent,
To *become* silence.

I thought I lost you!
Where have you been, dear stranger?
Nice to see my self!

With so many years
Of being at beck and call
I forgot to *be.*

The river was still
But I was not. Never mind:
The river was still.

Oh, to be that small
Boat on water! Waves rise, fall.
Small boat rises, falls.

In this quiet space,
Your face, Holy One, calms me.
Patiently waiting.

This world is too loud!
Sometimes I feel like saying,
Shut up, already!

To find silence, don't
Search for it. Just wait for it.
It will come to you.

Falling in a well
Of silence, how easily
I forget to leave.

It took me so long
To get here! A whole lifetime.
How can I leave now?

Away, for years…yet,
The key slips, easy, in lock
Opening silence.

Be still. Belong, still,
To this world, belonging to
Longing for the world.

Give thanks—more often.
Love yourself. Walk with others.
Wake up on the bridge.

Why does the green leaf
Tremble—yet not fall? Is it
Brave, or just foolish?

Sun, trees, river, wind.
I'd forgotten what it's like
To have a body.

God, Spirit, Light, Breath
Mystery flowing through us
Above, beyond— Near.

Inside, find that space.
Large, light, peaceful and ready.
Come. Enter. Be still.

Coming back to life,
After sleeping for so long,
I feel so alive!

Though I was awake,
I woke up, hearing this sound:
One bird, chirruping.

A wise saying goes,
Why bring a cup that is full
To the well? Good point.

Mindfully aging
Becoming an old woman
Day by day by day

Is this all there is?
Or do more years wait, hiding
On the other side?

Having reached half-way,
My body and soul are tired,
But mostly, grateful.

Endings, beginnings,
Long walks, roadblocks, getting lost:
Journeys, coming home.

Wherever you are,
Stop, look around. Breathe. Is this
Where you find yourself?

Slow down! Not so fast!
There's so much to see. Just think…
Of what you might miss.

Look, and look again.
Inside, out. Your life becomes just
One thing. One whole thing.

"So…are you happy?"
Sudden flock of birds—wings, flight.
Yes. I am happy.

The silence fills you.
You walk into not-knowing,
Knowing: all is well.

A book of haiku—
But…who will ever read it?
Kind reader: you did!

DEIRDRE CORNELL was born into a Catholic Worker family on the Lower East Side of Manhattan and grew up in Newburgh, New York and Waterbury, Connecticut. She received a BA in Anthropology from Smith College in Northampton, Massachusetts, and an MA in Theology from the Graduate Theological Union in Berkeley, California. She serves in pastoral and community settings, and has worked as a teacher.

Making their home in New York's Hudson River Valley, Deirdre, her husband, and their five children also spend time in Mexico. She is the author of three books (*A Priceless View, American Madonna* and *Jesus Was a Migrant*) and a spiritual life column. This is her first book of poetry.

www.ingramcontent.com/pod-product-compliance
Lightning Source LLC
Chambersburg PA
CBHW031221090426
42740CB00009B/1253